delicious.

Fresh

Who doesn't want lighter, brighter dishes...

... packed with flavour, texture and colour? *Fresh* is a handy collection of go-to guilt-free recipes to inspire easy mid-week dinners, sensational salads, vegetarian dishes and desserts that won't weigh you down. Fresh herbs, seasonal fruit, tangy dressings and lean protein bring these beautiful dishes to life so you don't have to sacrifice on flavour to eat well and feel good. And forget about expensive, hard-to-find ingredients, we've used everyday fruits and vegetables, meat, poultry and seafood, so you can eat well, every day.

Food is life, make it *delicious*.

delicious.com.au

Contents

Starters & Light Meals

Salads

Mains

Vegetarian

Sweet

Roasted tomato soup

1.5kg vine-ripened tomatoes,
  halved
2 onions, quartered
¼ cup (60ml) extra virgin
  olive oil
3 garlic cloves, chopped
2 tsp finely grated ginger
1 small red chilli, seeds
  removed, finely chopped
300ml tomato juice
800ml coconut milk
1 small bunch coriander,
  leaves and stems finely
  chopped, plus extra whole
  leaves to serve
1 tbs brown sugar
2 tbs fish sauce
Natural yoghurt and warm
  roti, to serve

Preheat the oven to 180°C. Line a baking tray with foil.

Place the tomato and onion on the baking tray and drizzle with 2 tablespoons olive oil. Season and roast for 1½ hours or until tomato and onion are very soft and lightly charred.

Meanwhile, heat remaining 1 tablespoon oil in a saucepan over medium heat. Cook the garlic, ginger and chilli, stirring, for 1–2 minutes until fragrant. Add the tomato juice, coconut milk and chopped coriander leaves and stems, then simmer for 6–8 minutes. Add the sugar, fish sauce, roasted tomato and onion, plus any cooking juices. Simmer for a further 2 minutes or until slightly thickened, remove from heat and allow to cool slightly.

Transfer the tomato mixture to a blender and blend until smooth. Season to taste.

Serve the soup either chilled or warm. Garnish the soup with coriander leaves, drizzle with yoghurt and serve with roti.
Serves 6–8

Thai chicken & pumpkin cakes

600g Jap or butternut
  pumpkin, peeled, chopped
1/3 cup (80ml) sunflower oil
1 bunch coriander
500g chicken mince
1 cup (70g) fresh breadcrumbs
3 kaffir lime leaves*, finely
  shredded
1 lemongrass stalk (inner core
  only), finely chopped
1 tbs Thai red curry paste
1 tbs fish sauce
2 garlic cloves, finely chopped
2 tsp sesame oil
Salad leaves, steamed rice,
  lime wedges and sweet
  chilli sauce, to serve

Preheat the oven to 180°C and line a baking tray with baking paper.

Place the pumpkin on the baking tray, drizzle with 1 tablespoon sunflower oil and season. Cover with foil, then bake for 25 minutes or until tender. Transfer to a large bowl, then mash with a potato masher or a fork until smooth. Allow to cool.

Finely chop the coriander roots, stems and leaves, then add to the cooled pumpkin with the chicken mince, breadcrumbs, kaffir lime leaves, lemongrass, curry paste, fish sauce and garlic. Mix well to combine, season, then shape into 12 thick patties. Chill for 15 minutes to firm up.

Place the sesame oil and remaining ¼ cup (60ml) sunflower oil in a frypan over medium-high heat. Cook the cakes for 1–2 minutes each side until browned, then place on a baking paper-lined baking tray and bake for 10 minutes or until cooked through.

Serve the chicken and pumpkin cakes with salad, rice, lime wedges and sweet chilli sauce. **Serves 4**

* Available from greengrocers and Asian food shops.

Beef tataki

300g piece centre-cut beef
  eye fillet, trimmed
2 tbs olive oil
2 tbs shichimi togarashi
  (Japanese spice mix)*
4 radishes, cut into
  matchsticks
¼ daikon (white radish), cut
  into matchsticks
1 small carrot, cut into
  matchsticks
Micro coriander or regular
  coriander leaves, to serve

Dressing
2 tbs soy sauce
1 tbs rice vinegar
1 tbs lime juice
½ tsp wasabi paste, plus
  extra to serve
1 garlic clove, crushed
1 tsp grated ginger
1 tsp caster sugar
½ tsp sesame oil

Brush the beef with 1 tablespoon oil, season, then coat in the shichimi togarashi. Place the remaining 1 tablespoon oil in a frypan over high heat. Cook the beef, turning, for 2–3 minutes until browned on all sides. Cool, then enclose the beef in plastic wrap and freeze for 1 hour (this will make it easier to slice).

Meanwhile, for the dressing, whisk all the ingredients together in a small bowl. Set aside.

Unwrap beef, then slice the beef wafer thin and place on a platter or individual serving plates. Scatter with the radish, daikon and carrot, then drizzle over the dressing. Garnish with coriander and serve with extra wasabi. **Serves 6**

* Available from Asian food shops and selected supermarkets.

Prawns with tomato ice cream

500g vine-ripened tomatoes

200ml thickened cream

1 tsp Worcestershire sauce

1½ tbs tomato paste

2 tsp caster sugar

1 small butter lettuce, leaves
separated

18 cooked prawns, peeled
(tails intact), deveined

¼ cup (50g) salmon roe

Basil leaves, to serve

Grate the tomatoes on the coarse side of a box grater and discard the skin. Press the grated tomatoes through a sieve, discarding the solids – you should have about 300ml tomato puree.

Whip the cream to soft peaks, then stir in the tomato puree, Worcestershire sauce, tomato paste and sugar. Season well.

Churn in an ice cream machine, according to manufacturer's instructions. Transfer to a plastic container and freeze for 3 hours or until firm.

To serve, divide the lettuce and prawns among serving bowls. Add a scoop of ice cream to each bowl, scatter with the salmon roe and basil leaves, then serve immediately. **Serves 4–6**

Spanish soup

2 tbs olive oil

1 onion, chopped

2 garlic cloves, finely chopped

3 carrots (about 500g),
  peeled, chopped

1½ tsp ground cumin

1 tsp sweet paprika

400g can chopped tomatoes

2 cups (500ml) chicken stock

¼ cup chopped flat-leaf
  parsley leaves

1 cup (250ml) dry sherry

Chopped hardboiled egg,
  curls of jamon* and small
  croutons, to serve

Heat the oil in a large saucepan over medium-low heat. Add the onion, garlic and carrot and cook, stirring, for 5–7 minutes until softened.

Add the cumin and paprika, stir well, then add the tomato and stock. Season with salt and pepper and bring to the boil. Reduce the heat to medium-low, partially cover and cook, stirring occasionally, for 18–20 minutes until the carrot is very tender.

Remove from the heat, then use a stick blender to puree the soup until smooth (or cool slightly, then puree in batches in a blender and return to the pan). Add the parsley and sherry, then warm through over low heat. Serve hot or chilled, garnished with egg, jamon and croutons, or serve the garnishes at the table in small bowls so everyone can help themselves. **Serves 4**

* Jamon is Spanish cured ham, available from selected delis, or use prosciutto.

Potted trout with dill cucumbers

250g hot-smoked trout, skin
   and bones removed
100g unsalted butter,
   softened, plus extra
   clarified butter to cover
½ tsp ground nutmeg
½ tsp ground mace*
   (optional)
1 tsp wholegrain mustard
Juice of 1 lemon
2 tbs chopped dill
Sliced baguette, to serve

Dill cucumbers
500g baby cucumbers (qukes)*
   or 4 small Lebanese
   cucumbers, thinly sliced
1 cup (250ml) white wine
1 cup (250ml) rice vinegar
250g caster sugar
6 dill sprigs
2 star anise
2 cloves
¼ tsp coriander seeds

For the dill cucumbers, place the cucumbers in a colander in the sink and liberally sprinkle with salt. Allow to drain for 30 minutes, then rinse well and place in a bowl. Place the remaining ingredients in a saucepan and bring to a simmer over medium heat, stirring until the sugar dissolves. Pour over the cucumbers and stand for at least 1 hour to pickle.

Place the trout, softened butter, spices, mustard, lemon juice and dill in a food processor, season, then whiz until you have a coarse pâté. Spoon into four ½ cup (125ml) ramekins or pots and cover with clarified butter. Chill for at least 30 minutes or until set. Remove from the fridge 30 minutes before serving.

Bring the potted trout back to room temperature, then serve with the drained dill cucumbers and baguette slices. **Serves 4**

* Mace is the lacy outer layer that covers the nutmeg seed, available from selected delis and Herbie's Spices (herbies.com.au). Baby cucumbers are available in season from greengrocers.

Vietnamese pork baguette

¾ cup (185ml) rice vinegar

½ cup (110g) caster sugar

2 carrots

½ daikon* (about 200g)

2 long red chillies, seeds removed, finely chopped

1 lemongrass stem (pale part only), finely chopped

2 garlic cloves, finely chopped

¼ cup (60ml) sunflower oil

450g pork fillet

2 tbs fish sauce

1 baguette

2 tsp soy sauce

3 tbs mayonnaise

¼ cup coriander leaves

¼ telegraph cucumber, thinly sliced

Place the vinegar, 4 tablespoons caster sugar and 100ml water in a small bowl. Add a pinch of sea salt, then stir until the sugar has dissolved. Cut the carrot and daikon into matchsticks (a mandoline is ideal), then add to the vinegar mixture and set aside for 2 hours to pickle. Drain.

In a large ceramic or glass dish, combine the chopped chilli, lemongrass, garlic and 2 tablespoons sunflower oil. Season the marinade with salt and pepper.

Slice the pork 1.5cm thick and lay between 2 pieces of plastic wrap or baking paper. Using a rolling pin, flatten out the pork slices until about 3mm thick, then place in the marinade, turning to coat. Cover and marinate in the fridge for at least 15 minutes.

Heat a wok or frypan over high heat and add the remaining 1 tablespoon sunflower oil. In batches, cook the pork for 1–2 minutes each side until browned and cooked through. Return all the pork to the pan, then add the fish sauce and the remaining sugar and cook for a few minutes until the pork is golden and caramelised.

Cut the baguette in half lengthways and brush the cut sides with soy sauce on one side and mayonnaise on the other. Fill the baguette with pork, cucumber, carrot, daikon and coriander leaves. Cut into quarters, tie with kitchen string, if desired, and serve immediately. **Serves 4**

* Daikon is a large white radish, from greengrocers and Asian food shops.

Caesar salad soup

6 pancetta slices

1 tbs olive oil

1 onion, chopped

1 garlic clove, chopped

1–2 anchovy fillets, chopped
(optional)

1 potato (about 200g), peeled,
chopped

3 cups (750ml) chicken stock

200g frozen peas

1 cos lettuce, outer leaves
discarded, thinly shredded

¼ cup (20g) grated parmesan,
plus extra to serve

2 tbs light sour cream

Toasted sourdough croutons,
to serve

Preheat the oven to 200°C.

Lay 4 slices of pancetta on a baking tray, then cover with a sheet of baking paper and top with another tray to keep it flat. Place in the oven and bake for 10 minutes until crisp, then break into shards and set aside to serve.

Meanwhile, heat the oil in a saucepan over medium heat. Chop the remaining pancetta and add to the pan with the onion, garlic and anchovy and cook for 2–3 minutes until the onion has softened. Add the potato and stock and bring to the boil, then reduce the heat to medium-low, cover and simmer for 10 minutes until potato has softened.

Add the peas and lettuce and simmer for 2 minutes until the lettuce has wilted. Remove from the heat and cool slightly. Stir in the parmesan and season, then use a stick blender to puree the soup until smooth (or cool slightly, then puree in batches in a blender and return to the pan). Warm through over low heat or serve chilled. Divide among bowls, drizzle with sour cream, then serve with crisp pancetta shards, croutons and extra parmesan.

Serves 4–6

Snapper ceviche

1kg skinless, boneless, red
snapper fillets, sliced
5mm thick
1 cup (250ml) lime juice, plus
extra lime wedges to serve
1 red onion, thinly sliced
1 roasted red capsicum*, cut
into thin strips
3 small red chillies, seeds
removed, finely chopped
½ cup chopped coriander
leaves
1 cup (250ml) extra virgin
olive oil
¼ cup (60ml) tequila (optional)
Crusty bread, to serve

Combine the fish and lime juice in a bowl (make sure the fish is
covered in the lime juice), then cover and marinate in the fridge for
4 hours (the lime juice will gently 'cook' the fish).

Drain off the marinade, then layer the fish in a glass serving bowl
or in a sealable jar (if picnicking), alternating layers with the onion,
capsicum, chilli and herbs, seasoning well between each layer.
Combine the oil and tequila, if using, then pour over the fish. Chill
for a further 30 minutes.

Serve with crusty bread, with lime wedges to squeeze over.
Serves 6.

* Available from delis.

Beef carpaccio with preserved lemon salad

600g piece beef eye fillet

1 cup (300g) whole egg
mayonnaise

1 tbs Worcestershire sauce

2 tbs milk

1 tbs lemon juice

2 tbs extra virgin olive oil

1 tbs baby capers, rinsed

½ bunch flat-leaf parsley,
leaves picked

¼ preserved lemon*, white
pith and flesh removed,
skin thinly sliced

Chill the beef in the freezer for 30 minutes so it will be easier to slice.

Meanwhile, whisk mayonnaise, Worcestershire sauce, milk and half the lemon juice together in a small bowl and season with salt and pepper.

Whisk oil and remaining lemon juice in a bowl, season, then add capers, parsley and preserved lemon and toss to combine.

Use a sharp knife to slice the beef fillet as thinly as possible. Place slices between sheets of baking paper, then gently roll with a rolling pin to make them thinner, without tearing.

Arrange the beef slices on a platter or individual plates. Scatter over the salad, then drizzle with the dressing and serve. **Serves 4–6**

* Available from gourmet food shops and delis.

French goat's cheese dip

300g soft goat's cheese*
1 tbs white wine vinegar
1 tbs dry white wine
2 tbs extra virgin olive oil
2 garlic cloves, crushed
2 tbs finely chopped flat-leaf
   parsley
2 tbs chopped chives
Baby (Dutch) carrots, celery
   sticks, radishes and crusty
   bread, to serve

Place the goat's cheese, vinegar, wine, oil, garlic, parsley and chives in a bowl with some sea salt and freshly ground black pepper. Beat well with a fork (or process in a food processor) until smooth, then serve with vegetables to dip and crusty bread. **Serves 4–6**

* If you're not a fan of goat's cheese, cream cheese works equally well.

Chilled cucumber soup with smoked trout tartines

30g unsalted butter, plus extra
   softened butter to spread
1 onion, chopped
4 telegraph cucumbers,
   peeled, seeds removed,
   chopped
200g pontiac or desiree
   potatoes, peeled, chopped
3 cups (750ml) chicken stock
3 dill sprigs, roughly chopped
200g creme fraiche 2 ficelle*
   loaves (or 1 baguette)
500g smoked trout, flaked
Mustard cress or rocket
   leaves, to garnish

Melt the butter in a saucepan over medium-low heat. Add the onion and cook, stirring, for 3–4 minutes until softened but not coloured. Add the cucumber, potato and stock, then season with salt and pepper. Bring to the boil, then simmer over medium-low heat for 20 minutes or until the potato is tender.

Cool slightly, then add the dill. Puree using a stick blender (or puree in batches in a blender) until smooth. Whisk in the creme fraiche and allow to cool. Cover and refrigerate for at least 4 hours until well chilled.

Just before serving, split the ficelle lengthways and spread with the softened butter. Fill with the smoked trout and season, then garnish with cress or rocket. Slice into 2–3 pieces each. Serve the chilled soup in bowls with trout tartines on the side. **Serves 4–6**

* A ficelle is a thin half-baguette available from selected bakeries.

Chicken rice paper rolls

150g rice vermicelli noodles

½ barbecue chicken

2 tbs sweet chilli sauce

1 tbs lime juice

¼ cup peanuts, chopped

12 x 22cm rice paper sheets*

1 Lebanese cucumber, cut
into thin matchsticks

2 tbs finely chopped mint

2 tbs finely chopped
coriander, plus extra leaves
to garnish

Dipping sauce

½ cup (110g) caster sugar

¼ cup (60ml) rice vinegar

1 tbs fish sauce

1 tbs sweet chilli sauce

2 small red chillies, finely
chopped

2 tbs finely chopped
coriander leaves

For the dipping sauce, place the sugar and vinegar in a pan with ¼ cup (60ml) water, then stir over low heat until the sugar dissolves. Cool slightly, then stir in the fish sauce, sweet chilli sauce, chopped chilli and coriander leaves. Set aside until needed.

Place the vermicelli noodles in a bowl and cover with boiling water. Set aside for 5 minutes to soften, then drain and rinse under cold water.

Shred the chicken meat, discarding the skin and bones, then place in a bowl with the sweet chilli sauce, lime juice, peanuts and drained noodles and gently toss to combine.

Fill a large, shallow bowl with hot water. Dip 1 rice paper sheet in the water for 30 seconds or until softened. Remove from the water, then place on a damp tea towel and allow to stand for 30 seconds until opaque and a little drier, but still pliable. Place some of the chicken mixture along the bottom third of the sheet, and top with some of the cucumber, mint and coriander. Fold the bottom edge of the rice paper up over the filling, then fold in the sides and roll up to enclose. Repeat to make 12 rolls.

To serve, garnish with coriander and drizzle with the dipping sauce. **Serves 4**

* Available from Asian food shops and selected supermarkets.

Ginger & chilli kingfish ceviche

300g sashimi-grade hiramasa
    kingfish*
½ red onion, thinly sliced
½ cup (125ml) lime juice (from
    about 3 limes)
1 garlic clove, crushed
1cm piece ginger, grated
1 long green chilli, seeds
    removed, finely chopped
3 coriander stems, finely
    chopped
Micro herbs or coriander
    leaves and unsprayed
    edible flowers* (optional),
    to serve

Enclose the fish in plastic wrap and freeze for 20 minutes (this will
make it easier to slice).

Meanwhile, soak the onion slices in a bowl of cold water for
10 minutes. Drain, then pat dry with paper towel. Set aside.

Place the lime juice, garlic, ginger, chilli and coriander stems in a
small bowl. Season, then whisk to combine.

Unwrap the fish, then very thinly slice and arrange on serving
plates. Drizzle with the lime dressing, then scatter over the onion.
Serve garnished with herbs and edible flowers, if desired. **Serves 6**

* Sashimi-grade hiramasa kingfish is available from fishmongers.
Edible flowers are available from farmers' markets and selected
greengrocers.

tuna tartare with crushed peas

½ garlic clove, finely chopped

1 tbs soy sauce

Pinch of caster sugar

2 tbs olive oil

1 tsp balsamic vinegar

2 tsp finely grated lemon zest

250g sashimi-grade tuna*, cut
into 2cm cubes

150g goat's curd*

Mustard cress* or snow pea
shoots, to garnish

Pea salad

1 cup (120g) frozen peas,
blanched

¼ cup (60ml) extra virgin
olive oil

1 tbs lemon juice

1 eschalot, finely chopped

1 tbs mint leaves, finely
chopped, plus extra leaves
to garnish

Place the garlic, soy sauce, sugar, olive oil, balsamic vinegar and lemon zest in a bowl, stirring to dissolve the sugar. Add the tuna and stir gently to coat in the mixture, then cover and marinate in the fridge for 15 minutes.

Meanwhile, for the pea salad, place most of the peas in a mortar or a bowl, reserving some whole peas to garnish, and gently crush with the pestle or a potato masher. Add the oil, lemon juice, eschalot and chopped mint. Season well with sea salt and freshly ground black pepper, then stir to combine.

Remove the tuna from the fridge and bring to room temperature, then remove the tuna from the marinade.

Spread one-quarter of the goat's curd onto each serving plate. Arrange the pea salad over the goat's curd, then top with cubes of marinated tuna. Garnish with the reserved whole peas, extra mint and mustard cress. **Serves 4**

* Sashimi-grade tuna is from fishmongers. Goat's curd is available from delis and gourmet food shops. Mustard cress is from selected greengrocers and supermarkets.

Scandi plate

6 slices rye or multigrain
   bread, toasted
300g beetroot dip
200g hot-smoked trout* or
   salmon, broken into pieces
½ cup creme fraiche or
   sour cream
3 tbs (50g) salmon roe*
   (optional)
1 punnet mustard cress*

Spread the warm toast with beetroot dip and place on serving plates. Break the fish into bite-sized pieces, discarding skin and bones, and place over the beetroot. Add a dollop of creme fraiche or sour cream, then top with salmon roe. Season with salt and pepper, scatter with the mustard cress and serve. **Serves 6**

* Hot-smoked trout is available from delis and supermarkets. Salmon roe is available from delis, gourmet food shops and fishmongers. Mustard cress is available from selected greengrocers and supermarkets.

Hot-smoked trout salad with horseradish cream

2 beetroots, trimmed,
  scrubbed
1 cup (220g) caster sugar
1 onion, thinly sliced
200ml white wine vinegar
200ml thickened cream,
  whipped to soft peaks
2 tsp lemon juice
¼ tsp dry mustard powder or
  1 tsp Dijon mustard
2 tbs horseradish cream
100g baby salad leaves or
  watercress
1 fennel bulb, thinly sliced
2 x 170g hot-smoked trout
  fillets*, flaked

Simmer beetroot in a pan of boiling, salted water until tender (this can take up to 1 hour).

Place all but 1 teaspoon sugar into a saucepan with 400ml water. Stir over low heat until the sugar dissolves. Add the onion and simmer for 3 minutes, then add the vinegar. Peel and slice the beetroot into rounds and add to the onion mixture, then remove from the heat and leave the beetroot to cool in the pickling liquid.

When ready to serve, combine the whipped cream, lemon juice, mustard, horseradish, remaining teaspoon of sugar and some salt and pepper in a bowl.

Strain the beetroot and onion from the pickling mixture and arrange on a plate with the salad leaves, fennel and the flaked salmon. Serve with the horseradish cream. **Serves 4**

* Hot-smoked trout is from supermarkets.

Melon, pecorino & prosciutto salad

1 long red chilli, seeds removed, very finely chopped
½ cup (125ml) extra virgin olive oil
¼ cup (60ml) vincotto*
½ honeydew melon
½ rockmelon
12 slices prosciutto, torn
125g shaved pecorino pepato*
Mint leaves, to serve

Combine chilli, oil and vincotto in a bowl and season. Set aside.

Cut the melons into thin slices and arrange on serving plates with the prosciutto. Scatter with the pecorino and mint, drizzle with the chilli dressing and serve. **Serves 6**

* Vincotto (substitute balsamic glaze) and pecorino pepato (a hard sheep's milk cheese studded with peppercorns) are available from Italian delis and gourmet food shops.

Vietnamese chicken salad

1 barbecued chicken, skin
  and bones discarded, meat
  shredded (to give 3 cups)
1 large carrot, cut into
  matchsticks
½ Chinese cabbage
  (wombok), shredded
½ red onion, thinly sliced
1 Lebanese cucumber, thinly
  sliced on an angle
1 long red chilli, seeds
  removed, cut into
  matchsticks
3 spring onions, thinly sliced
½ cup each Thai basil, mint
  and coriander leaves
1/3 cup (50g) chopped
  toastedpeanuts (optional)

Dressing
¼ cup (60ml) fish sauce
¼ firmly packed cup (50g)
  brown sugar
1 long red chilli (remove
  seeds for less heat),
  finely chopped
2 tsp grated fresh ginger
1 small garlic clove, chopped
100ml fresh lime juice

For the dressing, place the fish sauce and sugar in a small saucepan over low heat and cook, stirring, for 1–2 minutes until combined and the sugar has dissolved. Place in a blender with the chilli, ginger and garlic and blend until smooth. Stir in the lime juice and season with salt and pepper.

Combine the chicken, carrot, cabbage, onion, cucumber, chilli and most of the spring onion and herbs. Pour over half the dressing, toss well and divide among serving bowls. Garnish with peanuts, if desired, and remaining spring onion and herbs. Drizzle over the remaining dressing to serve. **Serves 4–6**

Greek lamb meatball salad

1/3 cup (80ml) olive oil

1 onion, finely chopped

4 garlic cloves, finely chopped

1 tbs ground cumin

1 tsp paprika

500g lamb mince

1½ cups (105g) fresh
    breadcrumbs

1 egg, lightly beaten

1 cup (280g) thick Greek-style
    yoghurt

Juice of 1 lemon

2 tbs finely chopped mint
    leaves, plus extra leaves
    to garnish

2 baby cos, leaves separated

2 roasted capsicums*, cut
    into strips

1 small telegraph cucumber,
    halved lengthways, sliced

½ cup mixed marinated olives

Heat 1 tablespoon olive oil in a frypan over medium heat. Add the onion and cook, stirring, for 2–3 minutes until softened. Add the garlic, cumin and paprika and cook for 30 seconds or until fragrant, then transfer to a large bowl and allow to cool. Once cool, add the lamb, breadcrumbs and egg, season well, then combine. With damp hands, form the mixture into 20 walnut-sized balls. Chill in the fridge for 30 minutes.

Preheat the oven to 180°C.

Heat 1 tablespoon oil in a large frypan over medium heat. In batches, cook the meatballs, turning, for 3–4 minutes until browned all over. Place on a large baking tray and bake in the oven for 6–8 minutes until cooked through.

Place the yoghurt in a bowl with 2 tablespoons lemon juice and 1 tablespoon chopped mint. Season with salt and pepper, then stir to combine.

Arrange lettuce, capsicum, cucumber and olives on a large serving platter or in individual bowls. Lightly whisk the remaining 2 tablespoons olive oil with the remaining lemon juice and chopped mint. Season to taste, then drizzle the dressing over the salad. Scatter the meatballs on top, drizzle with the yoghurt and garnish with mint leaves. **Serves 4**

* To roast capsicums, brush them with oil and then grill them on high for 3–4 minutes until the skins blister and blacken. Place capsicums in a bowl, cover with plastic wrap, then stand for 20 minutes until cool enough to handle. Remove and discard the skin, then slice capsicums into strips.

Prawn, white bean & chorizo salad

1 tbs olive oil

250g chorizo, sliced

12 green prawns, peeled
(tails intact), deveined

400g can cannellini beans,
rinsed, drained

250g punnet cherry tomatoes,
halved

½ red onion, thinly sliced

1 cup flat-leaf parsley leaves,
torn

½ cup mint leaves, torn

Dressing

1 garlic clove, crushed

1 tbs sherry vinegar or red
wine vinegar

⅓ cup (80ml) extra virgin
olive oil

Place the olive oil in a frypan over medium-high heat. Add the chorizo and cook, turning, for 2–3 minutes until crisp. Remove from the pan with a slotted spoon and drain on paper towel.

Add the prawns to the same frypan and cook for 1–2 minutes each side until just cooked. Set aside.

For the dressing, place all the ingredients in a bowl, season, then whisk to combine.

Place the beans, tomatoes, onion, parsley, mint, chorizo and prawns in large bowl. Add the dressing and toss to combine, then serve warm. **Serves 4**

Tomato couscous & salami salad

1 cup (250ml) tomato juice

1 cup (200g) couscous

2 tbs olive oil, plus extra
   to brush

12 slices peperoni

1 tsp grated lemon zest, plus
   2 tbs juice

½ tsp chilli flakes

100g wild rocket leaves

⅓ cup (50g) semi-dried
   tomatoes in oil, drained,
   finely chopped

120g bocconcini, cut into
   2cm cubes

Place the tomato juice in a saucepan over medium heat and bring to just below boiling point, then remove from the heat. Add the couscous and 1 tablespoon of the oil, then season with salt and pepper. Cover with a tea towel and stand for 10 minutes.

Place a chargrill or frypan over high heat. Brush the salami with a little extra oil and cook for 30 seconds each side until starting to crisp. Drain on paper towel.

Combine the lemon zest and juice, chilli flakes and remaining 1 tablespoon oil in a bowl and season with salt and pepper.

Use a fork to fluff the couscous grains. Add the rocket leaves, tomato, bocconcini, peperoni and the dressing and toss to combine. Pile the salad onto a serving platter. **Serves 4**

Tuna sashimi with wasabi bean salad

1–2 tsp wasabi paste (to
    taste), plus extra to serve

1 tbs red wine vinegar

2 tsp lemon juice

2½ tbs olive oil

350g thin green beans

1 small red onion, thinly sliced

Handful flat-leaf parsley
    leaves, torn

225g sashimi-grade tuna*,
    thinly sliced

Black* or regular sesame
    seeds, to sprinkle

Soy sauce, to serve

Combine the wasabi, vinegar and lemon juice in a bowl. Gradually whisk in the oil until well combined.

Slice the beans using an old-fashioned beaner (from kitchenware shops) or slice on an angle. Blanch in a pan of boiling salted water for 1 minute until just tender, then drain, refresh in cold water and drain again.

Toss the beans, onion and parsley in a bowl with the wasabi dressing. Divide the beans among small bowls, then place on serving plates with the tuna. Sprinkle with sesame seeds, then serve with soy sauce and a dab of extra wasabi. **Serves 4**

* Sashimi-grade tuna is from fishmongers. Black sesame seeds are from Asian food shops.

Goat's cheese, beetroot & praline salad

2 bunches baby beetroot (we
used golden* and regular)
or 850g can baby beets,
drained, halved
150g picked watercress
sprigs
250g soft goat's cheese,
crumbled
100g Vienna almonds*,
roughly chopped

Dressing
2 tbs white wine vinegar
1 tbs maple syrup
¼ cup (60ml) extra virgin
olive oil
1 tsp Dijon mustard

If using fresh beetroot, remove the leaves, leaving some stalk, and cook in boiling salted water for 25 minutes or until tender. Drain and refresh, then peel and halve.

Whisk all the dressing ingredients in a bowl and season with salt and pepper.

Lay the beetroot and watercress on a platter. Scatter over the goat's cheese. Drizzle with the dressing and scatter with chopped almonds. **Serves 4**

* Golden beetroot is available from selected greengrocers and growers' markets. Vienna almonds are available from nut shops and selected greengrocers. If you can't find them, use toasted almonds or pecans instead.

Japanese prawn, pickled vegetable & noodle salad

1 cup (250ml) brown-rice
   vinegar or regular
   rice vinegar
¼ firmly packed cup (50g)
   brown sugar
1 small carrot, cut into
   thin matchsticks
1 small cucumber, cut into
   thin matchsticks
250g soba or somen noodles
2 spring onions, cut into
   thin matchsticks
¼ cup each coriander and
   mint leaves
1 long red chilli, thinly sliced
1 cup snow pea sprouts,
   trimmed
20 cooked prawns, peeled,
   deveined
2 tsp toasted sesame seeds

Dressing
1 tbs honey
¼ cup (60ml) tamari or
   soy sauce
¼ cup (60ml) brown-rice
   vinegar or regular
   rice vinegar
¼ cup (60ml) olive oil
2 tsp sesame oil

Place vinegar and sugar in a small pan and stir over low heat until sugar dissolves. Increase heat to medium-high and simmer for 10 minutes or until syrupy, then allow to cool. Add the carrot and cucumber and set aside to pickle for up to 1 hour – the longer you leave them, the better they are.

Cook the noodles according to packet instructions, then drain. Place in a large bowl with the drained pickled vegetables, spring onion, herbs, chilli, snow pea sprouts and prawns.

For the dressing, whisk all ingredients together in a bowl. Add to salad and toss to combine. Sprinkle with sesame, then serve.
Serves 4

Burrata with prosciutto and peas

1½ cups fresh or frozen peas

⅓ cup (80ml) extra virgin
    olive oil

2 tbs lemon juice, plus lemon
    wedges to serve

1 cup (80g) finely grated
    parmesan

2 x 200g burrata balls*,
    roughly torn

8 thin prosciutto slices

⅓ cup small mint leaves

Chargrilled sourdough,
    to serve

Cook the fresh peas in a saucepan of boiling, salted water for 5–6 minutes (or 2–3 minutes for frozen) until tender. Drain, then refresh under cold water. Place in a bowl and roughly mash with a fork.

Whisk the olive oil and lemon juice together and season. Toss half the dressing with the peas, then stir through half the parmesan.

Divide half the peas among serving plates and top with burrata and prosciutto. Top with the remaining peas and drizzle with remaining dressing. Scatter with mint leaves and remaining parmesan. Season, then serve with chargrilled sourdough and lemon wedges. **Serves 4**

* This cheese with an outer layer of mozzarella and a soft creamy centre of unspun curds is available from Italian delis and specialist cheese shops. If you can't find it, use buffalo mozzarella instead.

Heirloom tomato salad with cheat's burrata

3 buffalo mozzarella balls
    (about 750g total), drained
2 garlic cloves, finely chopped
200ml creme fraiche
200ml thickened cream
1.2kg assorted heirloom
    tomatoes (such as Black
    Russian and Tigerella), or
    use vine-ripened tomatoes
2 loosely packed cups
    basil leaves
Extra virgin olive oil, to drizzle

Tear the mozzarella into large pieces. Toss in a bowl with the garlic, creme fraiche and cream, then season with sea salt and freshly ground black pepper. Set aside.

Slice the tomatoes and arrange on a platter or in a shallow serving bowl. Season and scatter with the basil leaves. Dot the mozzarella mixture over the salad and serve drizzled with extra virgin olive oil. **Serves 6**

Asian-style caprese salad

¼ cup (60ml) light olive oil

2 tbs rice vinegar

1 tbs soy sauce

2 tsp caster sugar

½ tsp sesame oil

300g packet silken firm tofu

4 vine-ripened tomatoes,
  sliced

2 tsp toasted sesame seeds

Thai basil leaves, to garnish

Combine olive oil, vinegar, soy, sugar and sesame oil in a small bowl, stirring to dissolve the sugar. To replicate the look of bocconcini or mozzarella slices, slice the block of tofu into 4 slices and use a 4cm pastry cutter to cut 2 rounds from each slice, discarding any excess (you could also simply cube the tofu to minimise any wastage).

Arrange the tomatoes and tofu on each serving plate. Drizzle with the dressing and scatter with sesame seeds and Thai basil.
Serves 4

Melon & blue cheese salad with citrus dressing

1 telegraph cucumber

½ rockmelon

2 cups watercress sprigs

½ red onion, thinly sliced

2 tbs thick Greek-style
yoghurt

175g soft blue cheese (such
as gorgonzola dolce), sliced

Citrus dressing

Juice of 2 oranges (about
½ cup)

1 tsp caster sugar

1 tsp lime juice

2 tbs lemon juice

¼ cup (60ml) olive oil

For the dressing, place the orange juice and sugar in a small saucepan over medium heat and simmer for 3–4 minutes until reduced by half (to about 3 tablespoons). Remove from the heat and add the lime juice and 1 tablespoon lemon juice. Slowly whisk in the olive oil, then season with salt and pepper. Set aside to cool completely.

Halve the cucumber, then thinly slice. Remove the skin and seeds from the rockmelon, then slice into wedges. Place the cucumber, melon, watercress and onion in a bowl and toss with half the dressing. Loosen yoghurt with the remaining 1 tablespoon lemon juice, then season to taste with salt and pepper.

Arrange the salad and gorgonzola on a platter or individual plates. Season, then drizzle with the remaining dressing and the lemon yoghurt. **Serves 4–6**

Vietnamese squid salad

750g small squid, cleaned (ask your fishmonger to do this)
100g Asian (red) eschalots*, thinly sliced
1 lemongrass stem (pale part only), thinly sliced
2 long red chillies, seeds removed, thinly sliced
2cm piece ginger, cut into matchsticks
3 spring onions, finely shredded
2 tbs chopped mint, plus extra to serve
3 kaffir lime leaves*, finely shredded
Handful Thai basil leaves*

Dressing
2 garlic cloves
2 small red chillies, finely chopped
Juice of 4 limes
1/3 cup (80ml) fish sauce
2 tbs brown sugar

For the dressing, place the garlic and chilli in a mortar and pestle and pound to a coarse paste. Place in a bowl, then stir in the lime juice, fish sauce and brown sugar. Set aside.

Cut each squid tube down 1 side and open into a flat piece. Score the inside with a diamond pattern, then cut each piece in half diagonally to form 2 triangles.

Bring a saucepan of salted water to the boil. In 3 batches, cook the squid pieces and tentacles for about 45 seconds until it curls up, making sure to return the water to the boil before cooking the next batch.

Place the hot squid in the bowl of dressing, then add the eschalot, lemongrass, chilli, ginger, spring onion and chopped mint and gently toss to combine. Divide the salad among plates, then garnish with extra mint, kaffir lime and Thai basil leaves. **Serves 6**

* Available from greengrocers and Asian food shops; substitute regular basil for Thai basil.

Chargrilled swordfish with tomatoes and olives

¼ cup (60ml) olive oil

1 red onion, finely chopped

3 garlic cloves, finely chopped

1 large rosemary sprig, leaves
  picked, finely chopped

½ tsp dried chilli flakes

400g cherry tomatoes, halved

¼ cup (60ml) red wine vinegar

2 tbs salted capers*, rinsed,
  drained

¾ cup (90g) green olives,
  pitted, chopped

1 tbs fresh oregano leaves,
  chopped

2 tbs chopped flat-leaf parsley

4 x 200g swordfish steaks

Crispy potatoes and rocket,
  to serve (optional)

Heat 1 tablespoon olive oil in a frypan over medium heat. Add the onion and cook, stirring, for 2–3 minutes until softened. Add the garlic, rosemary and chilli and cook for 30 seconds until fragrant. Add the tomatoes and cook for 3 minutes or until they begin to soften. Add the vinegar and allow to bubble for 2–3 minutes until evaporated. Stir in the capers, olives and oregano and parsley, season to taste, then cook for a further 2–3 minutes until heated through. Set aside.

Meanwhile, heat a chargrill pan or barbecue to medium-high heat. Brush the swordfish with the remaining 2 tablespoons oil and season well with salt and pepper. In batches if necessary, cook the swordfish for 1 minute each side or until seared but still rare in the centre. Divide the swordfish and crispy potatoes among plates, spoon over the tomato mixture, then serve garnished with rocket.
Serves 4

* Salted capers are available from delis and gourmet food shops.

Sumac lamb cutlets with fattoush

1 tbs sumac*
Juice of 1 lemon
½ cup (125ml) olive oil
2 garlic cloves, finely chopped
12 French-trimmed
    lamb cutlets
2 tsp Dijon mustard
2 tbs finely chopped
    mint leaves

Fattoush
12 cherry tomatoes, halved
1 round Lebanese bread,
    toasted, broken into pieces
100g marinated feta, drained
1 baby cos, leaves torn
1 cup mint leaves, plus extra
    to serve
1 cup flat-leaf parsley leaves
1 cup coriander leaves, plus
    extra to serve
1 cup mixed olives
1 Lebanese cucumber,
    chopped

Place the sumac, 1 tablespoon lemon juice, ¼ cup (60ml) oil and half the garlic in a glass or ceramic dish and season. Add the lamb cutlets, turning to coat in the marinade, then set aside for 30 minutes.

Meanwhile, place the mustard and remaining lemon juice and garlic in a bowl, then whisk to combine. Add the remaining oil in a slow, steady stream, whisking constantly, until you have a thick dressing. Season, then stir through the mint. Set aside.

For the fattoush, place all the ingredients in a large serving bowl and toss to combine. Set aside.

Preheat a barbecue or chargrill pan over high heat.

In batches if necessary, cook the lamb cutlets for 2–3 minutes each side for medium-rare or until cooked to your liking.

Toss the fattoush with half the dressing. Garnish the lamb cutlets with extra mint and coriander leaves, then serve with the fattoush and remaining dressing. **Serves 4–6**

* Sumac is a lemony Middle Eastern spice available from delis and selected supermarkets.

Rotelle with crushed peas, pancetta and mint

8 pancetta slices
250g vine-ripened cherry
    tomatoes
2 tbs olive oil, plus extra
    to toss
400g rotelle pasta
3 cups (360g) frozen peas
1/3 cup (80ml) pure (thin) cream
1 small bunch mint, leaves
    picked
1 cup (80g) grated parmesan

Preheat the oven to 180°C. Line 2 baking trays with baking paper.

Lay the pancetta slices on 1 tray. Place the tomatoes on the second tray, drizzle with the oil and season with salt and pepper. Place both trays in the oven (with the pancetta on top) and cook for 8–10 minutes until the pancetta is crisp and tomatoes begin to soften.

Meanwhile, cook the pasta according to packet instructions. Drain, then return to the pan, toss in a little oil and keep warm.

Cook the peas in boiling salted water for 3 minutes until tender, then drain.

Place 4 pancetta slices in a food processor with half the peas. Add the cream and half each of the mint and parmesan, then pulse briefly to crush – you want it to be quite coarse. Add the pea mixture to the pasta along with the remaining peas, then return the pan to low heat and toss for 1 minute to warm through.

Divide the pasta among bowls, tear over the remaining pancetta and top with roasted tomatoes, and remaining mint and parmesan.
Serves 4

* Rotelle are pasta wheels, available from delis and gourmet shops.

Moroccan salmon with preserved lemon dressing

2 tsp ground coriander

2 tsp ground cumin

1 tsp paprika

½ tsp ground turmeric

2 garlic cloves, roughly
   chopped

1 tbs lemon juice

¼ cup coriander, plus extra
   to garnish

¼ cup (60ml) olive oil

4 skinless salmon fillets,
   pin-boned

2 bunches asparagus,
   trimmed

Preserved lemon dressing

2 tbs chopped preserved
   lemon

½ cup (150g) whole-egg
   mayonnaise

2 tbs creme fraiche or
   sour cream

2 tbs chopped coriander

Place the spices, garlic, lemon juice, coriander leaves and ¼ cup (60ml) olive oil in a blender and blend to form a smooth paste. Season well, then coat the fish in the marinade. Cover and marinate in the fridge for 30 minutes.

Meanwhile, for the preserved lemon mayonnaise, combine the ingredients in a bowl, then cover and chill until needed.

Blanch the asparagus in boiling salted water for 2–3 minutes until just tender. Drain, then refresh in cold water. Set aside.

Heat a lightly oiled large frypan or barbecue to medium-low heat. Add the salmon and cook for 4 minutes each side or until golden (but still rare in the centre). Divide the asparagus among serving plates, top with the salmon, then drizzle with the mayonnaise and garnish with extra coriander. **Serves 4**

Tagliatelle with cheat's meatballs and cherry tomatoes

600g pork & herb sausages,
    casings removed
1 tbs olive oil
250g punnet cherry
    tomatoes, halved
¼ cup basil leaves, finely
    chopped, plus extra basil
    leaves to serve
400g tagliatelle or other
    long pasta
½ cup (40g) finely grated
    parmesan

Pasta sauce*
1.5kg vine-ripened tomatoes
¼ cup (60ml) extra virgin
    olive oil
2 garlic cloves, finely chopped
1 basil sprig
Pinch of caster sugar

For the pasta sauce, cut a cross in the base of each tomato and place in a large bowl. Pour over enough boiling water to cover, then stand for 30 seconds. Drain, then refresh immediately in a bowl of iced water. Once cool enough to handle, carefully peel, then cut into quarters, discarding the cores and seeds. Place the oil in a saucepan over medium-low heat. Cook the garlic, stirring, for 30 seconds or until fragrant, then add the tomato, basil sprig and sugar. Reduce heat to low, then simmer, stirring occasionally, for 30–40 minutes until the tomatoes have broken down and sauce is thick. Remove basil and season.

Meanwhile, roll the sausage meat into 3cm balls, then chill for 30 minutes to firm up.

Place the oil in a deep frypan over medium heat. Cook the meatballs, turning, for 3–4 minutes until browned. Add the pasta sauce and tomatoes, season, then reduce heat to low and simmer for 5–6 minutes until sauce is slightly reduced and the meatballs are cooked through. Stir through the chopped basil.

Meanwhile, cook the pasta according to the packet instructions until al dente. Drain, then add to the sauce and toss well to combine.

Divide the pasta and meatballs among shallow bowls. Sprinkle over the parmesan, then serve garnished with basil leaves. **Serves 4**

* If you don't have time to make the sauce, use a 600g jar of good-quality pasta sauce instead.

Poached chicken with warm Asian vinaigrette

4 x 170g chicken breast fillets
1 jasmine green tea bag
1 cup (200g) jasmine rice
½ cup (125ml) rice wine
  vinegar
¼ cup (60ml) soy sauce
¼ cup (60ml) mirin (Japanese
  rice wine)*
¼ cup (60g) grated dark palm
  sugar* or dark brown sugar
2 tbs sesame oil
3cm piece ginger, cut into
  very thin matchsticks
1 cup shredded spring onions
Micro herbs or coriander
  leaves, to serve

Place the chicken in a saucepan, cover completely with cold water and 1 teaspoon salt, then bring to the boil. Cover, then remove from heat and stand for 30 minutes or until chicken is cooked through.

Meanwhile, place the tea bag in a saucepan with 2½ cups (625ml) boiling water. Remove from the heat, then allow to steep for 15 minutes. Remove the tea bag, then add 1 teaspoon salt and bring back to the boil. Add the rice and cook according to the packet instructions, then drain.

Place the vinegar, soy sauce, mirin, sugar and sesame oil in a small saucepan over medium-low heat, stirring to dissolve the sugar. Stir in the ginger and ½ cup spring onion, then remove from heat.

Remove the chicken from the poaching liquid and thickly slice. Spoon the jasmine rice onto plates, top with the chicken and drizzle with warm vinaigrette. Garnish with herbs and the remaining ½ cup spring onion, then serve. **Serves 4**

* Available from selected supermarkets and Asian food shops.

Seared sesame tuna with soba noodles

1 tbs sunflower oil

400g centre-cut sashimi-
   grade tuna*

¼ cup (35g) white sesame
   seeds

¼ cup (35g) black sesame
   seeds*

200g soba noodles*

1 cup blanched soy beans
   (edamame)*

1 Lebanese cucumber, cut
   into wedges

1 punnet snow pea sprouts,
   trimmed

1 avocado, sliced

4 spring onions, sliced
   on an angle

Pickled ginger*, to serve

Dressing

2 tsp caster sugar

1 tsp wasabi paste

⅓ cup (80ml) ponzu (citrus
   soy)*

2 tbs mirin (Japanese rice
   wine)*

2 tsp fish sauce

Juice of 1 lime

Heat the oil in a frypan over high heat. Add the tuna and sear
for 1 minute on each side – you want the tuna to remain rare on the
inside. Allow to cool slightly.

Combine the sesame seeds on a clean chopping board and
roll the cooled tuna in the seeds to completely coat. Enclose tuna
tightly in plastic wrap, twisting ends to secure. Chill in the fridge
for 30 minutes.

For the dressing, combine all the ingredients and set aside.

Cook the soba noodles according to packet instructions, adding
the soy beans for the final minute, then drain and refresh.

Meanwhile, remove the tuna from the fridge and slice 5mm thick.

Toss the noodles and soy beans with the cucumber, sprouts,
avocado, spring onion and dressing. Divide among serving
plates, then top with tuna slices and garnish with pickled ginger.

Serves 4–6

* Sashimi-grade tuna is available from fishmongers. All other
ingredients are available from Asian food shops and
selected supermarkets.

Chicken schnitzel with avocado and pink grapefruit

4 cups (280g) fresh
   breadcrumbs
½ cup (40g) grated parmesan
1 tbs chopped thyme leaves
4 tbs chopped flat-leaf parsley
½ cup (75g) plain flour
2 eggs, lightly beaten
4 x 150g chicken breast
   fillets, flattened slightly
2 ruby grapefruits
2 avocados, flesh sliced
1 baby cos or butter lettuce,
   leaves separated
2 tsp Dijon mustard
2 tsp white wine vinegar
⅓ cup (80ml) extra virgin
   olive oil
Sunflower oil, to shallow-fry
Chopped chives, to sprinkle

Place the breadcrumbs, parmesan, thyme and parsley in a shallow bowl. Season with salt and pepper and combine well.

Place the flour and egg in separate dishes. Dip the chicken fillets firstly into the flour, shaking off excess, then into egg and finally in breadcrumb mixture, pressing to adhere. Chill in the fridge for about 10 minutes while you make the salad.

Meanwhile, peel the grapefruit and remove the pith, then slice the flesh into segments over a bowl to catch any juices. Arrange the grapefruit segments, avocado and lettuce on serving plates.

Whisk together the mustard, vinegar and olive oil in a bowl with 1–2 tablespoons of the reserved grapefruit juice to taste. Season with salt and pepper and use to dress the salad.

Heat 1–2cm sunflower oil in a large frypan over medium heat. Fry the schnitzels for 3–4 minutes each side until golden and cooked through.

Slice the schnitzel thickly, then arrange on the salad and serve sprinkled with chives. **Serves 4**

Smoked trout burgers with asparagus tzatziki

1 bunch asparagus, woody
  ends trimmed
1 egg
2 x 170g skinless hot-smoked
  ocean trout portions*
1¼ cups (85g) fresh
  wholemeal breadcrumbs
Grated zest and juice of
  1 lemon
2 tbs chopped mint leaves
200g thick Greek-style
  yoghurt
2 garlic cloves, crushed
2 tbs olive oil
4 wholemeal rolls or
  hamburger buns,
  split, toasted
Watercress sprigs and lemon
  wedges, to serve

Cook asparagus in boiling salted water for 2 minutes, then drain and refresh in cold water. Remove and reserve the tips. Chop the stalks, then place in a food processor with the egg. Blend until well combined. Add trout, breadcrumbs, lemon zest and juice, and half the mint and pulse to combine. Season to taste with salt and pepper. Using damp hands, form the mixture into 4 patties. Cover and chill for 30 minutes.

Shred the asparagus tips using a sharp knife, then fold into the yoghurt with the garlic and remaining mint. Season well, then cover and chill the asparagus tzatziki until required.

Heat the oil in a frypan over medium-high heat. Cook the trout patties for 2 minutes each side or until golden brown. Fill the toasted buns with tzatziki, patties and watercress, then serve with lemon wedges. **Serves 4**

* Available from supermarkets and delis.

Sushi rice bowl

2 cups (440g) brown rice

Grated zest and juice
   of 1 orange and 1 lemon

2 tbs caster sugar

2 tbs Japanese shoyu*
   or regular soy sauce

2 tbs brown-rice vinegar*
   or regular rice vinegar

400g firm tofu, patted dry,
   cut into 2cm cubes

1 tbs sunflower oil

4 sheets nori seaweed*

4 spring onions, sliced
   on the diagonal

1 small Lebanese cucumber,
   sliced into long, thin strips

1 avocado, sliced into
   thin wedges

50g snow pea sprouts, ends
   trimmed

Black sesame seeds*, toasted
   white sesame seeds and
   pickled ginger (gari)*,
   to serve

Cook the rice in boiling salted water according to packet instructions. Drain and allow to cool.

Meanwhile, place the citrus zest and juice in a saucepan with the sugar over medium-high heat. Stir to dissolve the sugar, then boil for 1 minute. Remove from the heat and stir in the shoyu and vinegar. Stir half the dressing into the cooled rice.

Heat a chargrill pan or frypan over medium heat. Brush the tofu with the oil and cook for about 1 minute, turning, until golden on all sides.

Line 4 serving bowls with the nori. Divide the rice among serving bowls, then top with the spring onion, cucumber, avocado and snow pea sprouts. Drizzle with the remaining dressing then sprinkle with sesame seeds and ginger. Serve with the chargrilled tofu.

Serves 4

* From Asian food shops and selected supermarkets.

Salmon with spiced carrot sauce

350ml fresh carrot juice

1 tbs Thai red curry paste

2cm piece ginger, peeled,
 sliced

1 lemongrass stalk (inner core
 only), bruised

2 kaffir lime leaves*, plus
 extra shredded kaffir lime
 leaves to serve

1 garlic clove, bruised

Finely grated zest and juice
 of 1 orange

1 tsp caster sugar

Juice of 1 lime

½ cup (125ml) coconut milk

2 tbs sunflower oil

4 x 180g skinless salmon
 fillets, pin-boned, cut into
 3cm pieces

Steamed rice, thinly sliced red
 chilli and micro coriander or
 coriander leaves, to serve

Place the carrot juice, curry paste, ginger, lemongrass, kaffir lime leaves, garlic and orange zest in a saucepan over medium heat. Bring to a simmer, then cook for 3 minutes. Cover, then remove from the heat and stand for 20 minutes to infuse.

Return the saucepan to medium heat. Add the sugar and orange and lime juices, stirring until the sugar dissolves. Strain into a clean saucepan, discarding the solids, then season and stir in the coconut milk. Gently warm over low heat.

Meanwhile, place the sunflower oil in a frypan over medium-high heat. Season the salmon, then cook, turning, for 4 minutes or until almost cooked through, but still a little rare in the centre.

Divide the steamed rice among deep bowls. Top with the salmon and ladle over the spiced carrot sauce. Serve garnished with chilli, coriander and shredded kaffir lime leaves. **Serves 4**

* Available from greengrocers.

Pork & prawn rissoles with fennel & rose petal salad

500g lean pork mince

8 large green prawns, peeled

1 tsp ground cumin

1 red onion, grated

4 garlic cloves, finely chopped

½ tsp dried chilli flakes

½ bunch coriander, leaves
  picked

¼ cup (60ml) olive oil

2 baby fennel bulbs,
  thinly sliced

6 radishes, thinly sliced

2 tbs dried edible rose petals*

1 tbs lemon juice

Place the pork mince, prawn meat, ground cumin, onion, garlic, chilli and most of the coriander into a food processor, reserving some coriander leaves for garnish. Pulse until just combined (don't over-process – you want the mixture to have some texture). Form into 12 patties, then chill for 30 minutes.

Preheat the oven to 180°C.

Heat 1 tablespoon oil in a frypan over medium-high heat. In batches, cook the patties for 2 minutes each side until golden, then place on a baking tray and cook in the oven for 6 minutes or until cooked through.

Combine the fennel, radish and rose petals in a bowl. Add the lemon juice and remaining olive oil, season with salt and pepper, then gently toss to combine.

Divide the patties among plates, then serve with the salad.

Serves 4

* Available from gourmet food shops and delis, or at herbies.com.au.

Baked whole salmon with wasabi tartare

2 eggs

1 garlic clove

½ tsp wasabi paste

Zest and juice of 1 lime, plus
 1 lime sliced

⅔ cup (165ml) light olive oil

2 tbs baby capers, rinsed

8 cornichons (small pickled
 cucumbers), roughly
 chopped

½ bunch coriander, leaves
 roughly chopped

1 small whole salmon or
 ocean trout* (about 2kg),
 filleted, skin removed,
 pin-boned

200g creme fraiche

2 cups mixed baby herb and
 salad leaves

Pulse the eggs, garlic, wasabi and lime zest in a food processor. Season with salt and pepper. With the motor running, add oil in a slow steady stream until you have a thick sauce. Add capers, cornichons, coriander and 1 tablespoon of lime juice (or more to taste), then pulse to combine.

Preheat the oven to 180°C.

Line a large baking tray with baking paper. Place a fillet on the tray, skinned-side down. Spread with half the sauce (reserving the rest to serve), then lay the lime slices down the length of the fillet. Top with the remaining fillet, skinned-side up. Cover with a sheet of baking paper, then enclose the fish completely in foil. Bake for 45 minutes, then remove and stand, still wrapped in foil, for a further 10 minutes to finish cooking. Test to see if the fish is cooked by gently pressing at the thickest part of the flesh – it should flake easily (cover with foil for a little longer if needed). Remove the foil and paper and carefully slide the salmon onto a serving platter. Stand for 15 minutes to cool to room temperature, or refrigerate until ready to serve.

Fold the creme fraiche into the reserved sauce.

Scatter the fish with herb and salad leaves, then serve with the sauce. **Serves 10–12**

* Order from fishmongers and ask them to fillet the salmon for you.

Tomato, goat's cheese & poppyseed tartines

250g punnet vine-ripened
   cherry tomatoes
2 garlic cloves
1 tsp chopped tarragon
1 tsp brown sugar
1 tbs balsamic vinegar
¼ cup (60ml) olive oil, plus
   extra to brush
120g soft goat's cheese
1 tbs milk
1 tbs poppyseeds
4 sourdough bread slices
Mint leaves, to serve

Preheat the oven to 160°C.

Divide the tomatoes into 4 bunches and place on a baking tray. Slice 1 garlic clove and place in a bowl with the tarragon, sugar, vinegar and oil, then whisk to combine. Season, then drizzle over the tomatoes. Roast for 30 minutes or until the tomatoes are soft and starting to split.

Meanwhile, place the goat's cheese, milk and poppyseeds in a bowl, season well and stir to combine. Set aside.

Preheat a barbecue or chargrill pan over high heat.

Brush the bread with oil, then grill for 1–2 minutes each side until charred. Halve the remaining garlic clove, then rub bread with the cut side of the garlic.

Spread the bread with the goat's cheese mixture and top with the tomatoes. Drizzle over the tomato roasting juices and serve garnished with mint. **Serves 4**

Steamed eggplant with tofu and snow peas

1 large eggplant, cut into
   3cm chunks
100g snow peas, trimmed
½ cup (125ml) Chinese black
   (chinkiang) vinegar*
⅓ cup (80ml) Chinese rice
   wine (shaohsing)*
3 garlic cloves, finely chopped
2 tbs brown sugar
2 tbs light soy sauce
1 tsp sesame oil
1 tbs grated ginger
⅓ cup (80ml) vegetable stock
   or water
250g silken firm tofu, cut into
   3cm cubes
2 tbs toasted sesame seeds
Steamed rice, to serve

Place the eggplant in a steamer over a pan of boiling water and steam for 10 minutes until tender, adding the snow peas for the last 2 minutes of cooking.

Meanwhile, place the vinegar, wine, garlic, sugar, soy sauce, oil, ginger and stock or water in a deep frypan over low heat. Cook, stirring, for 2 minutes or until the sugar has dissolved.

Add the steamed eggplant and snow peas to the frypan with the tofu, then toss gently to combine. Garnish with sesame seeds and serve with steamed rice. **Serves 4**

* Available from Asian food shops.

Spaghetti with peas, lemon and chilli

400g spaghetti or other
  long pasta
1½ cups fresh or frozen peas
3 long red chillies, seeds
  removed, finely chopped
300ml thickened cream
2 cups basil leaves, torn
1 cup mint leaves, torn
1 bunch chives, chopped
Finely grated zest and juice
  of 1 lemon
⅔ cup (100g) pine nuts,
  toasted
Finely grated parmesan and
  extra virgin olive oil,
  to serve

Cook the pasta in a saucepan of boiling, salted water according to the packet instructions, adding the fresh peas for the final 5 minutes of cooking time (or 3 minutes for frozen). Drain.

Return the pasta and peas to the warm saucepan. Add the chilli, cream, herbs, lemon zest and nuts, then toss gently together until just combined. Add the lemon juice to taste, then season.

Divide the pasta among plates. Sprinkle with the parmesan and serve drizzled with olive oil. **Serves 4**

Chilled pea soup with wasabi cream

30g unsalted butter

1 onion, finely chopped

1 pontiac potato (about
200g), peeled, chopped

2½ cups (625ml) chicken or
vegetable stock

2 cups fresh or frozen peas

250g creme fraiche

1 tsp wasabi paste*

Wasabi peas* and chervil or
mint leaves, to serve

Melt the butter in a saucepan over medium-low heat. Add the onion and cook, stirring, for 1–2 minutes until softened. Add the potato and stock, bring to a simmer over medium-high heat, then cook for 10 minutes, adding the fresh peas for the final 5 minutes of cooking time (3 minutes if frozen) or until tender. Use a stick blender to puree the soup until smooth. (Alternatively, allow to cool slightly, then puree in batches in a blender.) Season, then stir in half the creme fraiche. Chill for 1 hour.

Place the wasabi and remaining creme fraiche in a bowl, stirring to combine.

If necessary, adjust the consistency of the soup with a little water, then ladle soup into bowls or serving glasses, scatter with a few wasabi peas and top with a dollop of wasabi cream. Serve garnished with chervil or mint leaves. **Serves 4**

* From Asian food shops and selected supermarkets.

Heirloom tomato tarte fine

6 sheets frozen puff pastry,
    thawed
250g mascarpone cheese
⅔ cup (50g) finely grated
    parmesan
2 garlic cloves, finely chopped
2 tbs finely chopped basil,
    plus leaves to serve
6–8 brightly coloured
    heirloom tomatoes* (such
    as ox heart, yellow, kumato
    and green zebra) or
    vine-ripened tomatoes,
    halved, quartered or sliced
Olive oil, to drizzle

Cut a 15cm circle from each pastry sheet, then place the circles on 2 baking paper-lined baking trays. Using a fork, prick the pastry all over, then chill for 30 minutes.

Preheat the oven to 180°C.

Top the pastry with another sheet of baking paper, then weigh the pastry down with a second tray. Bake for 8 minutes or until golden and crisp. Set aside to cool completely.

Meanwhile, combine the mascarpone, parmesan, garlic and chopped basil in a bowl and season well with sea salt and freshly ground black pepper. Spread the cheese mixture over the cooled pastry bases. Arrange whole basil leaves and tomato on top, season to taste, then drizzle with olive oil. Serve immediately.

Serves 6

* Heirloom tomatoes are from selected greengrocers and growers' markets.

Baked ricotta & zucchini slice

3 pontiac or desiree potatoes
(about 600g), peeled

1½ tbs olive oil

6 bacon rashers, finely
chopped

2 zucchinis

2 eggs, lightly beaten

1kg fresh ricotta, well drained

¼ cup (20g) finely grated
parmesan

500g vine-ripened cherry
tomatoes

Small basil leaves and pesto*,
to serve

Preheat the oven to 180°C and grease a 25cm x 10cm loaf pan
or terrine.

Place the potatoes in a saucepan of cold, salted water. Bring to a
boil over medium-high heat, then cook for 8 minutes to par-boil.
Drain, cool, then coarsely grate into a large bowl.

Meanwhile, place 2 teaspoons oil in a frypan over medium-high
heat. Add the bacon and cook, stirring, for 2–3 minutes until crisp.
Drain on paper towel, then add to the grated potato.

Coarsely grate the zucchinis, then enclose in a muslin cloth or
clean Chux and squeeze to remove excess liquid. Add the zucchini
to the potato mixture with the eggs, ricotta and parmesan, then stir
well to combine. Season well.

Spread the ricotta mixture into the loaf pan. Bake for
25–30 minutes until puffed and golden. Cool for 10 minutes
in the pan.

Increase the oven to 220°C.

Place the tomatoes in a roasting pan, drizzle with the remaining
1 tablespoon oil and season. Roast for 10 minutes or until softened
and starting to collapse.

Turn out the baked ricotta onto a chopping board and cut into
2cm-thick slices. Serve warm or at room temperature with roasted
tomatoes, basil leaves and a dollop of pesto. **Serves 6–8**

* To make your own pesto, place a large bunch of basil (leaves
picked), 3 tbs pine nuts, 2 garlic cloves, ⅔ cup (50g) freshly grated
parmesan and ⅔ cup (50g) freshly grated Pecorino Romano in a
food processor. Pulse to combine, then gradually add olive oil until
you have a luscious green sauce.

Apple & goat's cheese salad

1 Granny Smith apple

1 Pink Lady apple

Juice of 1 lemon

½ red onion

1 baby fennel

150g aged goat's cheese*

2 tbs extra virgin olive oil

½ tsp wholegrain mustard

2 tsp Dijon mustard

1 tsp truffle honey*, plus
    extra to drizzle

1 cup micro salad leaves*

Core and thinly slice the apples into rounds (a mandoline is ideal). Toss the apple slices with most of the lemon juice, reserving 2 teaspoons for the dressing, and set aside.

Slice the onion and fennel very thinly (a mandoline is ideal) and cut the cheese into 5mm slices. Set aside.

Whisk the oil, mustards, truffle honey and reserved 2 teaspoons lemon juice together until combined, then season and set aside.

Toss the salad leaves with a little of the dressing. Stack the apple slices, onion, fennel, goat's cheese and salad leaves in layers on serving plates. Drizzle with the remaining dressing and extra truffle honey and serve. **Serves 4**

* Aged goat's cheese (substitute regular firm goat's cheese) and truffle honey are available from selected delis. Micro salad leaves are available from farmers' markets and selected greengrocers.

Tropical fruit salad with green tea ice cream

½ cup (110g) caster sugar

1 lemongrass stem (inner core only), bruised

1 star anise

3cm piece ginger, peeled, bruised

1 kiwi fruit, sliced

1 dragon fruit, sliced

1 star fruit, sliced

1 mango, sliced

1 papaya, sliced

Unsprayed edible flowers* (optional), to serve

Green tea ice cream

1 cup (250ml) milk

2 egg yolks

2 tbs caster sugar

2 tbs green tea powder (matcha)*, mixed with ¼ cup (60ml) boiling water

2–3 drops green food colouring

300ml thickened cream, lightly whipped

For the ice cream, place the milk in a saucepan over medium heat and bring to just below boiling point. Remove from heat. Place the egg yolks and sugar in a bowl and beat with electric beaters until thick and pale. Pour the hot milk into the yolk mixture, stirring constantly, then pour into a clean saucepan over low heat. Cook, stirring constantly, for 4–5 minutes until thick enough to coat the back of a spoon. Cool slightly. Stir the green tea mixture and food colouring into the custard, then transfer to a bowl and cover the surface closely with a piece of baking paper. Chill for 30 minutes or until cold. Fold the whipped cream through the cooled custard, then churn in an ice cream machine according to the manufacturer's instructions. (Alternatively, pour into a shallow container and freeze for 2 hours or until frozen at the edges. Remove from the freezer and beat with electric beaters. Repeat the process 2–3 times.) Freeze for 4 hours or until firm.

Meanwhile, place the sugar, spices and 2½ cups (625ml) water in a saucepan over low heat, stirring until sugar dissolves. Simmer for 2 minutes, then cool.

Place the sliced fruits in a bowl and pour over the spiced sugar syrup. Stand for 30 minutes to macerate.

Garnish the fruit salad with edible flowers, if desired, and serve with the green tea ice cream. **Serves 4–6**

* Edible flowers are available from farmers' markets and selected greengrocers. Green tea powder (matcha) is available from Asian food shops.

Pineapple carpaccio with sour cream ice cream

2 tbs white sugar

1 cup mint leaves, plus extra
  leaves to serve

½ vanilla bean, split, seeds
  scraped

1 small or ½ large pineapple,
  peeled, cored

Edible flowers* (optional), to
  serve

Sour cream ice cream

2½ cups (600g) sour cream

1 cup (220g) caster sugar

1 tbs glucose syrup*

Finely grated zest and juice
  of 1 small lemon

For the sour cream ice cream, place all the ingredients in a bowl and beat together with a wooden spoon. Stand for 20 minutes to allow the flavours to develop, then transfer to an ice cream machine and churn according to the manufacturer's instructions. (Alternatively, pour the mixture into a shallow container and freeze for 2 hours or until frozen at the edges. Remove from the freezer and beat with electric beaters, then return to the freezer. Repeat the process 2–3 times.) Freeze for 4 hours or until firm.

Place the white sugar, mint leaves and vanilla seeds in a mortar and pestle, then pound until the mint has broken up. Set mint and vanilla sugar aside.

Cut the pineapple lengthways into wedges, then very thinly slice (a mandoline is ideal).

Arrange the pineapple on plates, then serve with the sour cream ice cream, mint and vanilla sugar, extra mint leaves and edible flowers, if desired. **Serves 6–8**

* Edible flowers are available from farmers' markets and selected greengrocers. Glucose syrup is available from the baking aisle in supermarkets.

Coeur a la crème with strawberry & sumac granita

250g cream cheese, at room
   temperature
250g fresh ricotta
1 vanilla bean, split,
   seeds scraped
½ cup (75g) icing sugar, sifted
200ml thickened cream
Mint leaves, to serve

Strawberry & sumac granita
500g strawberries, plus extra
   quartered strawberries
   to serve
1 tbs lemon juice
½ cup (110g) caster sugar
2 tsp sumac*

Begin this recipe a day ahead.

For the granita, place the strawberries, lemon juice and caster sugar in a food processor and whiz to a smooth puree. Pass through a sieve, pressing down with the back of a spoon to extract as much juice as possible and discarding the solids. Stir in the sumac. Pour into a shallow plastic container, then freeze for 2 hours or until partially frozen. Remove the container from the freezer and break up the crystals by scraping the surface with a fork. Return to the freezer for 1 hour, then remove and scrape crystals again. Repeat this process twice more, then freeze overnight.

Meanwhile, pulse the cream cheese, ricotta, vanilla seeds and icing sugar in a food processor to combine. Add cream and pulse again. Line 4 coeur a la creme moulds* with muslin or clean Chux, fill with the ricotta mixture, then fold over muslin to enclose. Place on a wire rack set over a baking tray and chill overnight.

Remove the cremes from the fridge 10 minutes before serving, then unmould onto serving plates. Garnish with mint leaves and extra strawberries, then serve with the granita. **Serves 4**

* Sumac is a lemony Middle Eastern spice available from delis and selected supermarkets. Coer a la creme moulds are available from kitchenware shops. Alternatively, tie the mixture up in muslin to form little bundles.

Coconut ice ice-creams

⅔ cup (60g) desiccated
coconut
1 cup (220g) caster sugar
½ tsp coconut extract* or
vanilla extract
1 cup (250ml) sweetened
condensed milk
1L (4 cups) coconut milk
300ml thickened cream
150g coconut ice
confectionery*, broken
into pieces
Thinly sliced seasonal fruit
(such as plums or peaches),
to garnish

Place the desiccated coconut, caster sugar, coconut extract and condensed milkin a blender, then blend until combined. Transfer to a bowl and stir in the coconut milk. Using electric beaters, beat the cream to soft peaks, then fold into the coconut mixture. Churn in an ice cream machine according to manufacturer's instructions. Alternatively, pour the mixture into a shallow container and freeze for 2–3 hours until frozen at the edges. Remove from the freezer and beat with electric beaters, then refreeze. Repeat this process 2 or 3 times.

While the mixture is still soft, divide among eight ½ cup (125ml) dariole moulds or cups, then freeze until firm.

Meanwhile, place the coconut ice in a food processor and process to fine crumbs. Spread the coconut ice on a plate.

Run a warm knife around the edge of each mould, then turn out and roll in the coconut ice. Refreeze until needed, or serve immediately with sliced fruit. **Makes 8**

* Coconut extract is available from delis and gourmet food shops. Coconut ice is from sweet shops, or use extra desiccated coconut and a few drops of pink food colouring.

Hibiscus strawberries with yoghurt sorbet

1 cup (220g) caster sugar
1 vanilla bean, split,
   seeds scraped
250g jar hibiscus flowers
   in syrup*
2 x 250g punnets
   strawberries, hulled, halved
   if large

Yoghurt sorbet
½ cup (110g) caster sugar
500g thick Greek-style
   yoghurt
½ cup (125ml) milk

For the sorbet, place the sugar in a pan with ½ cup (125ml) water and stir over low heat until the sugar dissolves. Allow to cool slightly, then chill for 1 hour. Once it's completely cold, whisk in the yoghurt and milk, then churn in an ice cream machine according to the manufacturer's instructions. Alternatively, pour the mixture into a shallow container and freeze for 2 hours or until frozen at edges. Remove and beat with electric beaters. Return to the container and refreeze. Repeat 2 or 3 times.

To make the hibiscus strawberries, place sugar, vanilla bean and seeds in a pan with 1 cup (250ml) water and stir over low heat until the sugar dissolves. Simmer over medium-low heat for 10 minutes or until slightly reduced. Allow to cool, then stir in the flowers and syrup. Add the strawberries and leave to infuse for 30 minutes before serving in 6 glasses or small bowls, topped with a small scoop of the sorbet. **Serves 6**

* Hibiscus flowers in syrup are from gourmet food shops (we used Essence of Wild Hibiscus from Nicholson Fine Foods, visit: nicholsonfinefoods.com.au).

Blueberry & apple jellies

5 gold-strength gelatine
  leaves*
1 litre (4 cups) blueberry and
  apple juice
¼ cup (60ml) Calvados*
4 tbs low-fat thick Greek-
  style yoghurt
Fresh blueberries, to serve
Dried apple slices (optional),
  to decorate

Soak the gelatine leaves in cold water for 5 minutes to soften.

Place the juice in a saucepan over medium heat and bring to a simmer. Squeeze the excess water from the gelatine leaves. Add the gelatine to the pan with the Calvados and stir well. Remove from the heat and set aside to cool. Pour the mixture into 4 glasses or bowls, cover with plastic wrap and place in the fridge until firm.

Serve the jellies topped with yoghurt and fresh blueberries

Serves 4

* Gelatine leaves are available from gourmet food shops; always check the packet for setting instructions. Calvados is a dry apple brandy, available from selected bottle shops.

Coconut ice cream with lime & mint syrup

2 cups (140g) shredded
   coconut
1L coconut ice cream*
Tropical and seasonal fruits
   (such as kiwifruit, star fruit,
   papaya and mango), sliced,
   to serve

Lime & mint syrup
1 cup (220g) caster sugar
Grated zest of 2 limes
1/3 cup mint leaves, plus
   sprigs to garnish

Toast the shredded coconut in a dry frypan over medium-low heat, stirring, for 1–2 minutes until golden. Remove from the pan and cool.

Scoop the ice cream into balls, roll in the toasted coconut to coat and freeze on a lined baking tray for about 1 hour until firm.

Meanwhile, to make the lime and mint syrup, place the sugar, lime zest, mint leaves and 1 cup (250ml) water in a saucepan over medium heat. Stir until the sugar dissolves, then bring to a simmer and cook for 3 minutes or until slightly thickened and syrupy. Remove from the heat and set aside to cool, then strain and discard the lime zest and mint leaves.

Serve the ice cream balls on a platter with the fruit, mint leaves and a little syrup poured over. **Serves 6**

* Available from delis and ice cream shops. Substitute good-quality vanilla ice cream.

Quick strawberry tarts

375g block frozen puff pastry,
    thawed
1 egg, beaten
3 tsp caster sugar
½ cup (160g) strawberry jam
1 cup (250g) mascarpone
    cheese
1 vanilla bean, split,
    seeds scraped
¼ cup (40g) icing sugar,
    sifted, plus extra to dust
250g punnet strawberries,
    sliced
Orange zest strips and baby
    basil leaves (optional),
    to garnish
Flowers (optional), to decorate

Preheat the oven to 200°C.

Roll the pastry out on a lightly floured workbench to 3–5mm thick, then cut six 12cm x 5cm rectangles. Place on a lined baking tray and brush with the egg. Sprinkle with the caster sugar and top with another sheet of baking paper. Place another baking tray on top to keep the pastry flat. Bake for 15 minutes until crisp and golden. Set aside to cool.

To make a strawberry sauce, warm the jam in a saucepan over low heat, then press through a sieve, discarding any solids. Set aside.

Place the mascarpone, vanilla seeds and icing sugar in a bowl and beat until smooth.

When ready to serve, place the pastry rectangles on 6 serving plates and spread with mascarpone mixture. Top with strawberry slices and drizzle over the sauce, then sprinkle with orange zest, and baby basil and flowers if desired. Serve dusted with icing sugar.
Makes 6

Peach Melba buttermilk puddings

5 titanium-strength gelatine
   leaves *
600ml thickened cream
1 cup (220g) caster sugar
2 tsp vanilla extract
400ml buttermilk
4 ripe yellow peaches
2 x 125g punnets raspberries

Soak 3 gelatine leaves in cold water for 5 minutes to soften.

Place the cream, sugar, vanilla and buttermilk in a saucepan over medium heat, stirring to dissolve the sugar. Squeeze excess water from the gelatine, then add the gelatine to the cream mixture, stirring to dissolve. Strain the mixture through a fine sieve into a jug, then cool slightly and pour into 6 serving glasses. Cover and refrigerate for 3 hours or until set.

Meanwhile, cut a small cross in the base of each peach and place in a bowl. Pour in enough boiling water to cover the fruit and stand for 1 minute. Drain, then peel the peaches. Chop the peach flesh, discarding the stones. Place the flesh in a blender and puree until smooth, then pass through a sieve, dressing down to extract the juice. Discard the solids and set the peach puree aside.

Meanwhile, soak the remaining 2 gelatine leaves in cold water for 5 minutes to soften. Warm the peach puree in a saucepan over low heat. Squeeze excess water from the gelatine, then add the gelatine to the puree. Remove from heat and stir to dissolve the gelatine.

Cool, then pour the puree over the set buttermilk puddings and refrigerate for a further 2 hours or until set.

Garnish puddings with the raspberries and serve. **Serves 6**

* Gelatine leaves are available from gourmet food shops.

Mango risotto with tropical fruit

½ cup (110g) caster sugar

1 vanilla bean, split,
   seeds scraped

2 star anise

1 tbs finely grated lemon zest

1 tbs finely grated orange zest

25g unsalted butter

1 cup (220g) arborio rice

2 mangoes, chopped

150ml coconut cream, plus
   extra to serve

Tropical fruit and toasted
   coconut flakes, to serve

Place the sugar in a saucepan over low heat with the vanilla pod and seeds, star anise, citrus zest and 1L (4 cups) water. Stir to dissolve the sugar. Increase heat to medium-low and simmer for 5 minutes.

In a separate saucepan, melt the butter over low heat and add the rice, stirring for 1 minute to coat the grains. Add the sugar syrup and simmer for 30–40 minutes, stirring occasionally, until the rice is al dente. Cool slightly.

Meanwhile, place the mango flesh in a food processor and process until a smooth puree. Stir the puree and coconut cream through the risotto.

Serve the mango risotto warm or chilled with the tropical fruit. Drizzle with extra coconut cream and garnish with coconut flakes.
Serves 4–6

Index

Pork & prawn rissoles with fennel & rose petal salad 88
Prawns with tomato ice cream 12
Prawn, white bean & chorizo salad 46
Preserved lemon salad 24
Pumpkin cakes 8
Quick strawberry tarts 120

Rice paper rolls, chicken 30
Rissoles, pork & prawn 88
Roasted tomato soup 6
Rotelle with crushed peas, pancetta and mint 70

Salad
  Apple & goat's cheese salad 104
  Asian-style caprese salad 60
  Burrata with prosciutto and peas 56
  Fennel & rose petal salad 88
  Goat's cheese, beetroot & praline salad 52
  Greek lamb meatball salad 44
  Heirloom tomato salad with cheat's burrata 58
  Hot-smoked trout salad with horseradish cream 38
  Japanese prawn, pickled vegetable & noodle salad 54
  Melon & blue cheese salad with citrus dressing 62
  Melon, pecorino & prosciutto salad 40
  Pea salad 34
  Prawn, white bean & chorizo salad 46
  Preserved lemon salad 24
  Tomato couscous & salami salad 48
  Vietnamese chicken 42
  Vietnamese squid salad 64
  wasabi bean salad 50
Salami, salad with tomato and couscous 48
Salmon with spiced carrot sauce 86
Sashimi, tuna with wasabi bean salad 50

Sauces and dressings
  Asian vinaigrette 76
  Dipping sauce 30
  Preserved lemon dressing 72
  Seared sesame tuna dressing 78
  Spiced carrot sauce 86
  Vietnamese chicken salad dressing 42
  Vietnamese squid salad dressing 64
Scandi plate 36
Seafood – see Fish and seafood
Seared sesame tuna with soba noodles 78
Smoked trout burgers with asparagus tzatziki 82
Smoked trout tartines 28
Snapper ceviche 22
Snow peas, with tofu and steamed eggplant 94
Sorbet, yoghurt 114
Soup
  Caesar-salad soup 20
  Chilled cucumber 28
  Chilled pea soup with wasabi cream 98
  Roasted tomato 6
  Spanish soup 14
Sour cream ice cream 108
Spaghetti with peas, lemon and chilli 96
Spanish soup 14
Steamed eggplant with tofu and snow peas 94
Strawberry & sumac granita 110
Sumac lamb cutlets with fattoush 68
Sushi rice bowl 84

Tagliatelle with cheat's meatballs and cherry tomatoes 74
Tarte fine, heirloom tomato 100
Tartines, smoked trout 28
Tarts, strawberry 120
Thai chicken & pumpkin cakes 8
Tofu, with steamed eggplant and snow peas 94
Tomato couscous & salami salad 48
Tomato, goat's cheese & poppyseed tartines 92

Tropical fruit salad with green tea ice cream 106
Trout, potted with dill cucumbers 16
Tuna sashimi with wasabi bean salad 50
Tuna tartare with crushed peas 34
Tzatziki, asparagus 82

Vietnamese chicken salad 42
Vietnamese pork baguette 18
Vietnamese squid salad 64
Vinaigrette, Asian 76

Wasabi bean salad 50
Wasabi cream 98
Wasabi tartare 90
White bean, salad with prawn and chorizo 46

Yoghurt sorbet 114

The ABC 'Wave' device is a trademark of the
Australian Broadcasting Corporation and is used
under licence by HarperCollins*Publishers* Australia.

delicious. Fresh comprises recipes and photographs originally published in *delicious. Faking It* (2008),
delicious. Quick Smart Cook (2009), *delicious. More Please* (2010), *delicious. Simply the Best* (2011),
delicious. Home Cooking (2012) and *delicious. Love to Cook* (2013)

First published in Australia in 2016
by HarperCollins*Publishers* Australia Pty Limited
ABN 36 009 913 517
harpercollins.com.au

HarperCollins*Publishers*
Level 13, 201 Elizabeth Street, Sydney NSW 2000, Australia
Unit D1, 63 Apollo Drive, Rosedale Auckland 0632, New Zealand
A 53, Sector 57, Noida, UP, India
1 London Bridge Street, London, SE1 9GF, United Kingdom
2 Bloor Street East, 20th floor, Toronto, Ontario M4W 1A8, Canada
195 Broadway, New York NY 10007, USA

Little, Valli, author.
 Delicious : fresh / Valli Little.
 ISBN: 978 0 7333 3452 8 (paperback)
 Includes index.
 Subjects: Cooking.
641.5

Photography by Brett Stevens, Ian Wallace, Jeremy Simons
Styling by David Morgan, Louise Pickford
Cover and internal design by Hazel Lam, HarperCollins Design Studio
Layout by Sam Williams
Colour reproduction by Graphic Print Group, Adelaide SA
Printed and bound in China by RR Donnelley

5 4 3 2   16 17 18 19